THE POETRY OF CALIFORNIUM

The Poetry of Californium

Walter the Educator

Silent King Books

SILENT KING BOOKS

SKB

Copyright © 2024 by Walter the Educator

All rights reserved. No part of this book may be reproduced in any manner whatsoever without written permission except in the case of brief quotations embodied in critical articles and reviews.

First Printing, 2024

Disclaimer
This book is a literary work; poems are not about specific persons, locations, situations, and/or circumstances unless mentioned in a historical context. This book is for entertainment and informational purposes only. The author and publisher offer this information without warranties expressed or implied. No matter the grounds, neither the author nor the publisher will be accountable for any losses, injuries, or other damages caused by the reader's use of this book. The use of this book acknowledges an understanding and acceptance of this disclaimer.

"Earning a degree in chemistry changed my life!"
– Walter the Educator

dedicated to all the chemistry lovers, like myself, across the world

CALIFORNIUM

In the depths of Earth, where mysteries hide,

CALIFORNIUM

Californium slumbers, deep inside.

CALIFORNIUM

Amidst the rocks and the soil it dwells,

CALIFORNIUM

A silent witness to ancient tales it tells.

CALIFORNIUM

A synthetic element, created with care,

CALIFORNIUM

In laboratories, its secrets we dare.

CALIFORNIUM

A product of fusion, of atoms combined,

CALIFORNIUM

In nuclear reactors, its genesis defined.

CALIFORNIUM

Named for California, land of the west,

CALIFORNIUM

Where science and discovery manifest.

CALIFORNIUM

A tribute to pioneers, to those who strive,

CALIFORNIUM

In quest of knowledge, to keep hope alive.

CALIFORNIUM

Invisible to the naked eye, yet it gleams,

CALIFORNIUM

With radiation emitting its beams.

CALIFORNIUM

A source of power, of energy untamed,

CALIFORNIUM

In controlled environments, its essence is framed.

CALIFORNIUM

Its isotopes varied, with properties diverse,

CALIFORNIUM

Each one a marvel, a universe.

CALIFORNIUM

Decay and half-life, constants in flux,

CALIFORNIUM

In the dance of particles, they conduct.

CALIFORNIUM

From medical uses to weaponry's might,

CALIFORNIUM

Californium's applications take flight.

CALIFORNIUM

A tool for healing, for diagnosing woes,

CALIFORNIUM

Yet wielded in conflict, its darker shadow shows.

CALIFORNIUM

In the depths of space, in celestial spheres,

CALIFORNIUM

Californium whispers, in cosmic years.

CALIFORNIUM

Forged in supernovae, in stellar cores,

CALIFORNIUM

It journeys through galaxies, forevermore.

CALIFORNIUM

Its luminescence captivating the mind,

CALIFORNIUM

A muse for poets, a puzzle to find.

CALIFORNIUM

In the alchemy of words, its essence expressed,

CALIFORNIUM

In verse and rhyme, its story caressed.

CALIFORNIUM

From Berkeley's labs to far-flung lands,

CALIFORNIUM

Californium's legacy expands.

CALIFORNIUM

A testament to human ingenuity,

CALIFORNIUM

And the boundless depths of curiosity.

CALIFORNIUM

So let us marvel at this element rare,

CALIFORNIUM

In its complexity, in its flair.

CALIFORNIUM

For in its nucleus, a universe unfurls,

CALIFORNIUM

In Californium, the wonder of worlds.

CALIFORNIUM

ABOUT THE CREATOR

Walter the Educator is one of the pseudonyms for Walter Anderson. Formally educated in Chemistry, Business, and Education, he is an educator, an author, a diverse entrepreneur, and he is the son of a disabled war veteran. "Walter the Educator" shares his time between educating and creating. He holds interests and owns several creative projects that entertain, enlighten, enhance, and educate, hoping to inspire and motivate you.

Follow, find new works, and stay up to date
with Walter the Educator™
at WaltertheEducator.com

www.ingramcontent.com/pod-product-compliance
Lightning Source LLC
LaVergne TN
LVHW051921060526
838201LV00060B/4107